THE GHOST FILES

GHOSTLY ENCOUNTERS

by Suzanne Garbe

Consultant:
Dr. Andrew Nichols
Director
American Institute of Parapsychology
Gainesville, Florida

CAPSTONE PRESS
a capstone imprint

Edge Books are published by Capstone Press,
151 Good Counsel Drive, P.O. Box 669, Mankato, Minnesota 56002.
www.capstonepub.com

Library of Congress Cataloging-in-Publication Data
Garbe, Suzanne.
    Ghostly encounters / by Suzanne Garbe.
    p. cm.—(Edge books. The Ghost Files)
    Includes bibliographical references and index.
    Summary: "Describes several types of ghostly encounters and relates stories
that involve each type"—Provided by publisher.
    ISBN 978-1-4296-6515-5 (library binding)
    1. Ghosts—Juvenile literature. I. Title. II. Series.
BF1461.G37 2012
133.1'4—dc22   2011003788

Editorial Credits
Aaron Sautter, editor; Tracy Davies, designer; Svetlana Zhurkin,
        media researcher; Eric Manske, production specialist

Photo Credits
Alamy: Ace Stock Limited, 11, Paul Heartfield, 7; Corbis: Science Faction/Ed
Darack, 20; Dreamstime: Maximilian Buzun, 15; Fortean Picture Library, 5, 19,
23, 25 (both); Getty Images: Keystone-France/Gamma-Keystone, 17, Tea Shafie,
13; iStockphoto: Duncan Walker, cover, Greg Nicholas, 29; Mary Evans Picture
Library, 21; Newscom: Graham Morris, 27, Picture History, 9 (inset), Roll Call
Photos/Tom Williams, 9 (bottom)

Printed in the United States of America in Stevens Point, Wisconsin.
032011   006111WZF11

TABLE OF CONTENTS

CHAPTER 1

Encountering the Unexplained

Four friends gather in front of the bathroom mirror. "Have you ever heard of Bloody Mary?" asks one girl. Then she flips the light switch off, and the bathroom plunges into darkness.

"Bloody Mary!" she yells. "Bloody Mary! Bloody Mary!"

A faint light suddenly flickers in the mirror. One girl screams. Another one scrambles to open the door. Light floods the room. The friends look back in the mirror, but it shows only their own terrified faces.

If you've ever told a ghost story, you've shared in an ancient tradition. Ghosts have fascinated people for thousands of years. Of course, not everyone believes in them. Many skeptics think ghost reports have natural explanations or are simply tales made up to amuse or scare people. Some experts work hard to find logical reasons to explain reported ghostly activity.

skeptic – someone who questions things other people believe in

Did you see a ghostly figure moving in the shadows? Or was it just a trick of the light?

However, some people have had strange, unexplained experiences. Ghostly apparitions have been seen in many forms. These apparitions sometimes look like people. But they can look like other creatures such as dogs and horses. People have also reported seeing ghostly objects such as clothing, airplanes, and even buildings. Other scary encounters can take the form of unexplained lights or noises, or even flying furniture.

In the following pages, you'll learn about several people's strange and terrifying ghostly encounters. For these people, there's only one explanation. They believe ghosts are real—and that they're among us.

FACT According to one study from 2005, 32 percent of people in the United States believe in ghosts.

apparition – the visible appearance of a ghost

Each year, thousands of people report seeing ghostly apparitions and other strange activit

CHAPTER 2

HUMAN APPARITIONS

Perhaps the most commonly reported encounters involve human apparitions. Some of these spirits are seen only once. But others return again and again to the same location. Most are faint and transparent, while a few look as solid as living people. Some might moan or speak, while others are completely silent. No matter how they appear, an encounter with an apparition can be a chilling experience.

A RUINED REPUTATION

At first, Louise Mudd Arehart heard footsteps and knocks in her home. Then doors began opening and closing by themselves. Finally, the apparition of a man appeared. Louise recognized him as her dead grandfather, Dr. Samuel Mudd.

In 1865 Dr. Mudd was a key player in events surrounding the death of President Abraham Lincoln. After shooting Lincoln, John Wilkes Booth escaped with a broken leg. Dr. Mudd treated Booth's injury. Dr. Mudd claimed he didn't know what Booth had done. But he spent several years in prison for helping the killer anyway. For the rest of his life, Dr. Mudd was haunted by his ruined reputation.

After seeing her grandfather's ghost, Louise worked to clear his name. She also restored his home as a historical landmark. Louise didn't see her grandfather's ghost again. But some visitors to the house claim they've seen and heard Dr. Mudd's spirit. Perhaps he is still trying to prove his innocence.

DR. SAMUEL MUDD

Several people have reported seeing Dr. Mudd's ghost at his old home in Maryland.

THE GUARDIAN GHOST

One commonly reported human apparition is the guardian ghost. Guardian ghosts often save people's lives by warning them about dangerous situations. Melba Goodwyn is a paranormal researcher and writer. She believes guardian ghosts often try to protect children from harm.

Goodwyn's family once claimed to have an encounter with this kind of spirit. Her grandson, Michael, saw a mysterious boy jumping on his bed for three nights in a row. Each night, Michael's parents said the boy wasn't real and sent him back to his room.

FACT Some people believe children are more likely to see ghosts because they are more open to the supernatural.

paranormal – having to do with unexplained events

But on the third night, Michael was so scared that he slept on the couch. During the night, a driver crashed his car into the family's house—right into Michael's bed! Luckily, he wasn't sleeping there and was unhurt. Goodwyn believes the ghostly boy was real. She credits the guardian ghost with saving her grandson's life.

CHAPTER 3

CRISIS APPARITIONS

Human apparitions are usually reported long after a person's death. But crisis apparitions are different. In these reports, a person's ghost often appears to a loved one just moments after death. Occasionally, a spirit may appear at the exact moment of a person's death or just before death. Many people believe these spirits appear to say a final good-bye to their loved ones.

INDIA AND RAY

India and Ray had been very close since grade school. But when they were 16 years old, India's parents told her they were moving to another city. India and Ray promised they would write letters, visit often, and one day get married.

Unfortunately, they would never have the chance to marry. One night after India moved, a mysterious cloud entered Ray's bedroom. The cloud slowly turned into the image of India. Ray moved toward her, but she smiled sadly and disappeared before he could touch her.

The next day, Ray got the bad news. The previous night, India had been killed when a train struck her car. She had died at the exact moment Ray had seen her in his bedroom.

Ray was deeply saddened by India's death. But he was glad to have seen her ghost. Ray believed India had come for one last good-bye to comfort him when she died.

CHAPTER 4

NON-HUMAN APPARITIONS

Witnesses have reported non-human apparitions in many forms. People have claimed to see ghostly animals, vehicles, and even buildings. Skeptics think these events are simply tricks of the light or people's overactive imaginations. But whatever the cause, non-human apparitions can leave people spooked for years.

THE GUIDE DOG

Dr. Gaine Cannon once had a startling encounter with a ghostly dog. Cannon was a respected doctor who worked in the mountains of North Carolina. One day he heard about a girl he knew who was very sick. He decided to drive through a blinding snowstorm on dangerous mountain roads to help.

As Dr. Cannon drove through the storm, he couldn't find the road to the girl's house. He was lost, and he worried that he would arrive too late to help her. Suddenly he heard a dog barking.

He quickly recognized the family's dog. He stopped his car, turned around, and followed the dog through the trees. Finally, the girl's house appeared ahead. With relief, Dr. Cannon went inside. He had arrived in time to treat the sick girl.

Later, Dr. Cannon told the girl's mother how the dog guided him to the house. She gave the doctor a puzzled look. He was shocked when she said the dog had died several weeks earlier!

FACT When he was five years old, actor Keanu Reeves saw a strange sight. A white suit walked through his bedroom on its own power, with nobody inside. Then it disappeared!

World War II Airplanes

Ghostly apparitions of objects and people related to wars are often reported. People have reported seeing the ghosts of dead soldiers, military ships, and airplanes.

One day in 1995, Tony Ingle was walking his dog in the English countryside. He was surprised to see an old plane flying low in the sky. The propellers moved, but the plane didn't make a sound. Then it banked suddenly like it was going to crash. Ingle ran toward the crash site, but he found no sign of a wreck.

Ingle later learned that an identical plane had crashed at the same spot during World War II (1939–1945). Everyone on board was killed. Ingle realized that he must have seen an apparition of the downed airplane.

Several other people have reported ghost planes in the same area. In 1997 another plane appeared to crash—prompting a large rescue mission. However, no wreckage was ever found.

More than 300 people have died in plane crashes in the region. Many of the crashes are related to World War II. Some believers claim ghostly planes haunt the land because the dead passengers never received a proper burial.

FACT
Apparitions from the past are sometimes called "time slips." Some people think these sightings are a result of a person or object briefly traveling through time.

CHAPTER 5

GHOSTLY LIGHTS

Ghostly encounters don't always involve the appearance of people, animals, or objects. Some people believe ghosts can appear as strange, unexplained lights. Ghostly lights can appear in many shapes and colors. They appear most commonly as orbs, vortexes, and mists. Ghostly lights often have a natural explanation. But many people who see them believe the lights are evidence of ghosts.

THE MARFA LIGHTS

One night, Joe Skelton was driving down a dark road near Marfa, Texas. Suddenly, he saw bright, orb-shaped lights in his mirror. He panicked and thought a truck was coming up too fast behind him. But when he looked over his shoulder, there was no sign of a vehicle—and the lights had disappeared.

orb - a glowing ball of light connected to ghostly activity

Like many ghostly encounters, ghostly lights are sometimes linked to a particular place. Marfa, Texas, is one area famous for these odd lights. For more than 100 years, people have reported seeing strange, basketball-sized lights near Marfa. The strange lights have been reported floating over distant hills and in nearby fields. They've also been spotted throughout Big Bend National Park.

many people think the spooky lights near Marfa, Texas, are visible spirits of the dead.

vortex - a whirling mass of light connected to ghostly activity

Some people even believe the Marfa lights have interacted with them. Journalist Frank Tolbert claimed that whenever he tried to investigate the lights, they disappeared. And Mrs. W. T. Giddens has reported seeing the lights follow ranchers through their fields at night. Her father even said the lights once led him to safety during a blizzard.

Scientists suggest glowing minerals or methane gas may cause the lights. They also say the lights could simply be reflected natural light. But local legends claim that the lights are spirits of long-dead pioneers, bandits, or American Indians. In spite of many reported encounters with the lights, nobody knows the true reason for their appearance.

MARFA'S MYSTERY LIGHTS
VIEWING AREA
1 MILE

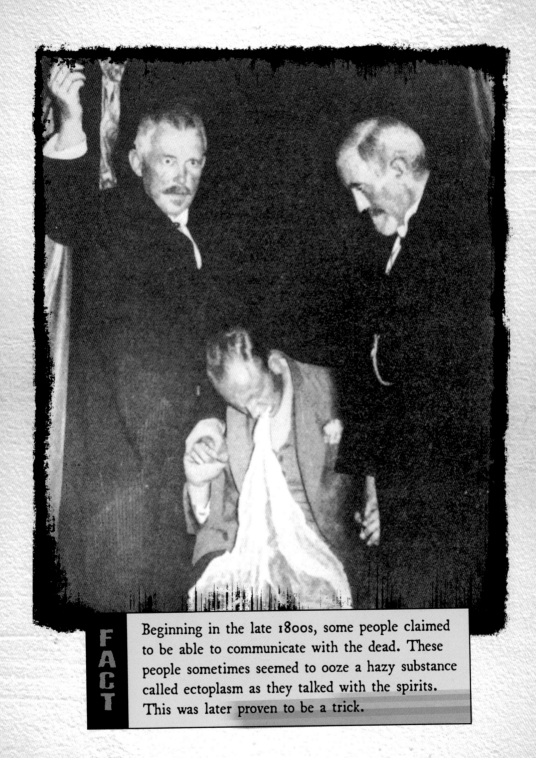

Beginning in the late 1800s, some people claimed to be able to communicate with the dead. These people sometimes seemed to ooze a hazy substance called ectoplasm as they talked with the spirits. This was later proven to be a trick.

CHAPTER 6

POLTERGEISTS

Poltergeists are famous for being mischievous. These spirits are almost never seen. Instead, poltergeist reports often include loud knocking sounds and other noises. Objects are often seen flying through the air for no obvious reason. Spoons might suddenly fly off the kitchen table. Or a heavy dresser will slide across the floor. Although poltergeists often scare people, they rarely cause physical harm.

Poltergeists are almost always linked to a certain person, rather than to a particular place. Poltergeist activity often occurs near teenagers who are going through great stress. Some researchers believe poltergeist activity is caused by psychic energy created by children as they grow into teenagers. Other people believe poltergeists are actual spirits. While nobody knows the true cause, poltergeist activity has been reported throughout the world.

mischievous – able or tending to cause trouble

Poltergeist activity often involves objects moving around a room by themselves.

psychic — having to do with a person's soul or mind

The Rosenheim Poltergeist

One of the most famous poltergeist stories happened in Rosenheim, Germany, in 1967. When 19-year-old Anne-Marie Schneider started her new job, life in the office changed dramatically. While she worked, lightbulbs popped and burned out. Employees picked up ringing telephones to find no one was on the line. Paintings rotated on the walls, and ink overflowed from copy machines.

Anne-Marie's boss brought in help from the phone company, the power company, and police officers. He even asked scientists and paranormal investigators for advice. In all, 40 people witnessed the strange events. But nobody had a good explanation.

They did discover one thing about the weird activity. All the events seemed to be linked to Anne-Marie. The poltergeist activity only happened when she was in the office.

Finally, after several months, Anne-Marie's boss fired her. The strange events stopped immediately. When Anne-Marie started a new job, milder poltergeist activity appeared there too. But it didn't last long. With nothing left to study, the investigators left the case unsolved.

ANNE-MARIE SCHNEIDER

Swaying lights, moving drawers, and other strange activity was often observed near Anne-Marie.

FACT After the Rosenheim story became well known, the number of Germans believing in poltergeists increased by about 50 percent.

THE ENFIELD POLTERGEIST

Enfield, England, is home to another famous poltergeist case. Eleven-year-old Janet Hodgson first noticed strange shuffling sounds and knocking in her room. Over the next several months, the strange activity got worse. Heavy furniture slid across floors without being touched. Doors opened on their own. Janet levitated off her bed. And curtains wrapped themselves around her neck as if to strangle her.

Skeptics tried to explain the events. They pointed out that Janet's parents had recently divorced and that her brother was suffering from cancer. Perhaps the stressful situations had given Janet psychic powers. Other people thought Janet had simply faked everything to get attention. However, the police officers, scientists, and journalists who saw the events swore everything actually happened.

After more than a year, Janet was placed in a hospital. Doctors studied her for several months. They found nothing unusual physically. When she returned home, the poltergeist activity soon stopped.

Nobody knows what really happened to Janet Hodgson. She still lives in England, but she rarely speaks about the case.

Pillows and other objects reportedly moved by themselves in Janet Hodgson's home.

What Do You Believe?

When people report seeing a ghostly figure,
are they coming face to face with a ghost? Or are
their own imaginations getting carried away?
What do you think? Are spooky lights and creepy
apparitions evidence of ghosts? Or are there
logical explanations for these strange events?

Whether you're a believer or a skeptic, you're
not alone. Many people have attempted to explain
the unknown. But nobody has discovered the full
truth about ghostly encounters—and perhaps
nobody ever will.

Photographs of human apparitions are
often explained as reflections of light
in a camera lens.

GLOSSARY

apparition (ap-uh-RISH-uhn)—the visible appearance of a ghost

levitate (LEV-i-tate)—to rise into the air without a natural cause

mischievous (MISS-chuh-vuhss)—able or tending to cause trouble

orb (AWRB)—a glowing sphere of light that sometimes appears in photographs taken at reportedly haunted locations

paranormal (par-uh-NOHR-muhl)—having to do with an unexplained event that has no scientific explanation

psychic (SYE-kik)—having to do with a person's soul or mind

skeptic (SKEP-tik)—a person who questions things that other people believe in

vortex (VOHR-tex)—a whirling mass of light connected to ghostly activity

READ MORE

Axelrod-Contrada, Joan. *Ghoulish Ghost Stories.* Scary Stories. Mankato, Minn.: Capstone Press, 2011.

Cotter, Charis. *A World Full of Ghosts.* New York: Annick Press, 2009.

Kuryla, Mary. *Ghost Files: The Haunting Truth.* New York: HarperCollins Publishers, 2008.

Wetzel, Charles. *Haunted U.S.A.* Mysteries Unwrapped. New York: Sterling, 2008.

INTERNET SITES

FactHound offers a safe, fun way to find Internet sites related to this book. All of the sites on FactHound have been researched by our staff.

Here's all you do:

Visit *www.facthound.com*

Type in this code: 978142965155

 Check out projects, games and lots more at **www.capstonekids.com**

INDEX